21st Century
Basic Skills
Library

KIDS CAN
REUSE

3

by Cecilia Minden, PhD

Cherry Lake Publishing • Ann Arbor, Michigan

CHERRY
LAKE
Publishing

Published in the United States of America
by Cherry Lake Publishing
Ann Arbor, Michigan
www.cherrylakepublishing.com

Photo Credits: Cover and page 1, ©iStockphoto.com/gchutka; page 4,
©studiots/Shutterstock, Inc.; page 6, ©ampyang/Shutterstock, Inc.;
page 8, ©Shmel/Shutterstock, Inc.; page 10, ©iStockphoto.com/
dlinca; page 12, ©Jacek Chabraszewski/Shutterstock, Inc.; page 14,
©iStockphoto.com/cstar55; page 16, ©Christina Kennedy/Alamy;
page 18, ©D. Hurst/Alamy; page 20, ©palmaria/Shutterstock, Inc.

Library of Congress Cataloging-in-Publication Data
Minden, Cecilia.
  Kids can reuse/by Cecilia Minden.
     p. cm.—(Kids can go green!)
  Includes index.
  ISBN-13: 978-1-60279-868-7 (lib. bdg.)
  ISBN-10: 1-60279-868-0 (lib. bdg.)
  1. Recycling (Waste, etc.)—Juvenile literature. 2. Environmental
Protection—Citizen participation—Juvenile literature. I. Title. II. Series.
  TD794.5.M56 2010
  628.4'458—dc22   2009049108

Cherry Lake Publishing would like to acknowledge
the work of The Partnership for 21st Century Skills.
Please visit www.21stcenturyskills.org for more information.

Printed in the United States of America
Corporate Graphics Inc.
July 2010
CLFA07

TABLE OF CONTENTS

What Can Kids Reuse?

To **reuse** means to use something in a new way.

Let's take a look around your room.

What can you reuse?

Look for things you no longer use. Be sure they are clean and in good shape.

Go through your **closet**. Sort your toys, games, and sports **equipment**.

Now look around the rest of your home.

What else did you find?

Newspaper, bags, and boxes can all be reused.

How Can Kids Reuse?

You can **donate** some of your things to **charity**.

Old clothing can be turned into quilts or cleaning rags.

Swap with your friends. What is old to you will be new to them.

Many reused things are good for **crafts**. Check your library for craft books.

Painted paper bags can be used to wrap gifts.

Small boxes can be used to **organize** little things.

Where Can Kids Reuse?

Talk to your family about ways everyone can reuse.

Help your class think of ways to reuse in the classroom.

Sometimes **neighbors** get together to have big yard sales.

They reuse and make money at the same time!

Reusing helps **reduce** the amount of trash in our **landfills**. Reducing trash is one way to keep Earth green.

What will you reuse today?

Find Out More

BOOK

Alter, Anna. *What Can You Do with an Old Red Shoe?: A Green Activity Book about Reuse.* New York: Henry Holt, 2009.

WEB SITE

U.S. EPA—Planet Protectors Club for Kids
www.epa.gov/waste/education/kids/planetprotectors/index.htm
Learn more about protecting Earth.

Glossary

charity (CHA-ruh-tee) an organization that helps raise money for people in need

closet (KLAHZ-it) a small room used to store things

crafts (KRAFTS) hobbies in which you create things with your hands

donate (DOH-nate) to give something to a charity as a gift

equipment (i-KWIP-muhnt) tools needed for a certain purpose

landfills (LAND-filz) places where garbage is piled up

neighbors (NAY-burz) people who live near one another

organize (OR-guh-nize) to arrange and store things neatly

reduce (ri-DOOSS) to make something smaller or less

reuse (ree-YOOZ) to use something again

Home and School Connection

Use this list of words from the book to help your child become a better reader. Word games and writing activities can help beginning readers reinforce literacy skills.

a	clothing	helps	no	shape	toys
about	craft	home	now	small	trash
all	crafts	how	of	some	turned
amount	did	in	old	something	use
and	donate	into	one	sometimes	used
are	Earth	is	or	sort	way
around	else	keep	organize	sports	ways
at	equipment	kids	our	sure	what
bags	everyone	landfills	painted	swap	where
be	family	let's	paper	take	will
big	find	library	quilts	talk	with
books	for	little	rags	the	wrap
boxes	friends	longer	reduce	them	yard
can	games	look	reducing	they	you
charity	get	make	rest	things	your
check	gifts	many	reuse	think	
class	go	means	reused	through	
classroom	good	money	reusing	time	
clean	green	neighbors	room	to	
cleaning	have	new	sales	today	
closet	help	newspaper	same	together	

Index

About the Author

Cecilia Minden is the former Director of the Language and Literacy Program at the Harvard Graduate School of Education. She currently works as a literacy consultant for school and library publishers and is the author of more than 100 books for children.